Foreword

We are delighted to introduce this compilation ~~~~~~~~~ illustrated as always by his paintings. Dad died last year at eighty, only seven months after our mother. As Dad came to the end of his life, he said that his prayers increasingly consisted of holding the person or problem wordlessly before God. Yet he retained a wonderful ability to put into writing the conversations he had with his God. His prayers have it all – the doubts and anxieties, the frustrations and anger, the longing and love and the quirky ability to come at things from an unexpected angle in a way that deepens our understanding.

Dad's enormous experience of life, the joyful and the painful, went into his writing. His prayers are accessible and strike chords for all of us. We were often surprised to find that things we had told him, and things that our children had said or done, went into his writings and were used to shed new light on life. He was someone very human working out his relationship with God and using all his God given abilities to do so.

Underneath it all was his belief that God was there, sometimes silent but always listening to him patiently and lovingly, if at times with a wry smile and an even more unexpected response.

Stephanie Bell and *Jenny Hawke*

Part One: Starting the Day

Cornish Afternoon – *Watercolour*

Lord of time and eternity,
I don't know what today may bring,
but I know you're just around the corner.
Thank you.

Lord, today is your gift to me.
Help me to turn it into my gift to you.
Each today pushes back the past into history,
and in the long perspective
I can see your hand at work.
For good. For my good.
And from that view
I can turn to face the prospect of today.

Today is my concern.
Good news in the present tense.
Not just for me, Lord –
although in honesty that's where my interest begins –
but for those with whom I live and work and talk.

Make me an instrument for good.
A small focus of your healing
in a worried world.

I thank you for yesterday.
I leave tomorrow in your hands.
Today is yours and mine.

Edge of the Lake – *Watercolour*

Lord, help me face the day.
Help me to seize the time
and shake it
'til the joy it holds
spills out
and fills my life.
Help me to sense your presence on the road,
and in those moments
when I seem alone
give me the faith that says you're there.

Lord of all joy,
let me see the good
in those I meet today.
And if it's hard to find,
to dig a little deeper 'til I do.

Lord, take the little I can give.
At times I hesitate
to offer it at all
my talent seems so small.
But if my loaves and fish can be of use
I offer them with joy.
Please take them,
and in your creative love
transform both them and me.

Water's Edge – *Watercolour*

Lord, I need you now.
Not as a refuge.
Not as a dream.
As a companion.
As someone to walk with me
on the road.

Golden Morning – *Watercolour*

Lord of today,
grant me the courage and strength
to stand and fight
for what my heart tells me
is true and good.

◆

Lord of all joy,
give me the courage
to step through the garden gate
and live today with you.

◆

Lord, life with you can be uncomfortable.
Keep me awake,
the excitement makes it all worthwhile.

Lord of life,
help me to live it well today,
and when the edges of my understanding
get a little frayed,
strengthen my faith.

◆

Lord of all beauty,
shine your light on me today
that I may brighten up the lives
of those I meet.

◆

Creator Lord,
you brought the world to order out of chaos.
Help me create a little order in my life today.

Part Two: Talking About Prayer

Patience – *Watercolour*

Sometimes, Lord, often –
I don't know what to say to you.
But I still come, in quiet,
for the comfort of two friends
sitting in silence.

Lord, teach me to pray
It sounds exciting, put like that.
It sounds real. An exploration.
A chance to do more than catalogue
and list the things I want,
to an eternal Father Christmas.

The chance of meeting you, of drawing closer to the love that
made me, and keeps me, and knows me.
And, Lord, it's only just begun.
There is so much more of you,
of love, the limitless expanse of knowing you.
I could be frightened, Lord, in this wide country.
It could be lonely, but you are here, with me.

The chance of learning about myself,
of facing up to what I am. Admitting my resentments,
Bringing my anger to you, my disappointments, my
frustration. And finding that when I do, when I stop struggling and
shouting and let go you are still there.
Still loving.

Sometimes, Lord, often –
I don't know what to say to you.
But I still come, in quiet, for the comfort of two friends
sitting in silence.
And it's then, Lord, that I learn most from you.
When my mind slows down, and my heart stops racing.
When I let go and wait in the quiet,
realizing that all the things I was going to ask for
you know already.
Then, Lord, without words, in the stillness
you are there ...
And I love you.

Lord, teach me to pray.

Lord, give me the wisdom
to know just when to pray
and when to act.
It's all too easy to confuse the two.

Sunlit Wood – *Watercolour*

When I pray
'Your kingdom come'
Inspire me
to share in its building

Filtering Sunshine – *Watercolour*

Lord, sometimes I'm afraid to pray.
It scares me,
this whole business of talking to you.
Listening to you.
Who am I ...?
And what does it mean?
It's a heavy thing, Lord,
to be in contact with you.
It would be all right
if I could just use the passkey,
open the letterbox,
drop in my requests,
like a mail-order catalogue,
and wait for the parcel to come.

But when I pray
I hear you talking back to me.
I hear you saying
"You've used the words.
Now what are you going to do about it?"
Confronting, searching.
I think of Jesus, in the garden.
I catch a glimpse of what prayer meant to him.

Sweat... like blood... Agonizing, painful.
Prayer from the depths of his being
whether for others or himself.
Prayer beyond easy words.
Commitment. To the cross. And beyond.

Lord, teach me to pray in His name. In His Spirit
Not only believing prayer.
Not simply believing you'll do something about it.
But identifying prayer. Putting myself into it,
standing alongside you, Lord,
and committing myself to do all I can
to bring about what I'm praying for.

Lord, help me.
When I pray for peace, help me not to create dissension.
When I pray for my neighbour, stir me up to help him.
When I pray 'Your kingdom come' inspire me to
share in its building.

Help me put my will where my mouth is,
and not to shift onto your shoulders
the things I can do something about myself.

Part Three: Needing Peace

Broken Fence – *Watercolour*

Give me the grace to pause,
take breath
and reassess just where I am,
find time to hear your voice in quiet.

So often, Lord,
I am a hamster on a treadmill.
Going round and round incessantly
and getting nowhere.
At least the hamster can get off
and curl up in a corner of his cage,
but when he does
he finds he's back where he began,
no progress made.
I know the feeling.
Running to stand still, my energy burnt up.
And in the busyness no time for you.
I don't think that's your will for me –
for any of us, come to that.
Even you, Lord, rested on the Sabbath day.

Give me the grace to pause,
take breath
and reassess just where I am,
find time to hear your voice in quiet.
I know there's so much to be done
but Earth will not implode if I sit down and rest.

The pillars of the kingdom
won't come crashing down
if I let go my grip and stop.
And in the silence
as the treadmill of my mind stops turning
I'll hear you offering me
Shalom.
The peace that passes understanding.
And then refreshed,
my energy restored,
I can begin again to live
as you would have me live.

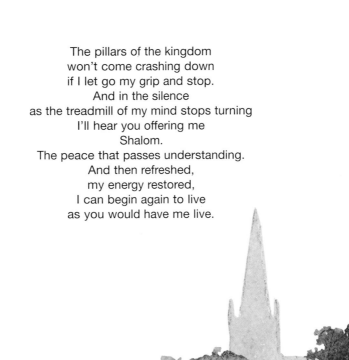

Lord, help me make a quiet place, a space
where you and I can meet at peace.
Where I can sit and wait, and listen.
A calm where loving eyes can meet and interlock.
Not frantic in haste,
a brief handwave from passing cars.
But in the slow contentment of two friends together.
Maybe no need even to speak the words
I love you.
You know I love you.
Because I give you time.

Lord, slow me down.
Take my foot off the accelerator
And guide it, gently, to the brake.
Cool my overheated mind, slow my heartbeat.
Tell me again, and again,
that the world, your world,
will quite possibly survive
without my frantic support.
Remind me that it's not my great endeavour
that keeps the earth's foundations firm.
But yours.

Frosty Morning – *Watercolour*

So easy, Lord, to crowd you out.
So much to do,
so little time to do it all.
I struggle through the crowd
of my own busyness to get to you,
each little thing an obstacle delaying me.
And everything I need to do
coils round my feet and trips me up.
Keeps us apart.

All that I need to do, Lord?
You question it –
why do I need to do so much?
Well then,
there's family and church
and all those other jobs
that fill my diary and ...
You question me again.
But all I do, I do for you, or try to anyway,
and if the quality's not very good
you could at least acknowledge
all the effort I put in.

But when I take a breath
and stop to think,
the very work I do for you
holds us apart.

And if I really love you,
as I say I do,
I'd push away the things
my ego thinks important
to spend more time
not working for,
but being with,
the one I say I love.
I think we'd both enjoy it more.

Part Four:
Coping with
Trouble and Worry

Lazy Afternoon – *Watercolour*

Lord, sometimes
my burdens seem too heavy
and my energy too light.
But if you'll take the other end
I'll try to lift my share.

Lord, I've felt alone
so many times.
Bruised black and blue by life.
The tiles blown off the roof
of my self-confidence
by the storm.
The cold rain of doubt poured in,
flooding my faith.

I've cried to you
in desperation and uncertainty
and no one's answered.
I've thought you were asleep,
or far away, or even worse
that you'd abandoned me.

I'm sorry, Lord
but in the gathering darkness of my fears
clouds blackening my horizon
can so quickly blind me to your presence.

The one thing I hang on to
each time the storm clouds gather,
is that you've graced my life
with mercy in the past
and so will come again to do the same.
Even there I've got it wrong.
How can you come again when you're already here,
whatever doubt may tempt me to assume?

Just help me face the wind and wait.
I know you'll show yourself
and still my storm
just when I need you most.

Winter Sun – *Watercolour*

Shine in my darkness, Lord.
Dispel the doubt and fear
that cling so close.
Turn the weak moonlight of my faith
to brighter day
in which I see your radiance,
know your love.

◆

Lord, when I'm puzzled, uncertain,
help me to remember
you're in control.
Your finger on the button.
And, whether I can see the end or not,
help me to accept
that you know where we're going.

Lord, whatever I may say, I have it easy.
You know I've got problems –
you should, I spend most of my prayer time
telling you about them; and often, forgive me,
telling you exactly how I want them solved.
But when I look around with eyes and mind open
and see what others have to face
then I know – I have it easy.

There are folk around me with bigger problems
than mine.
Frightened, anxious and lonely,
wanting a little bit of human contact.
Needing a little courage to face
problems and hang on to life.

A.D. ASKEW

I can encourage them
just by being with them, just by listening.
Just by taking off a bit of their load, like you take mine.
Is that what you want me to do?
I can't do it on my own – but thank you, Lord.
I don't have to.

Lord, it's good to know you are with me,
in all the strains life brings.
In the disappointments and difficulties
let me feel your presence.
And, Lord, help me to share this with others.
Make my presence with them your presence.
May your Spirit in me encourage and strengthen.
And as I recognize Jesus walking beside me,
may others see something of him in me.
Lord, thank you,
because you are always here.

A.D. ASKEW

Passing Shower, Norfolk – *Watercolour*

Lord, what I really want is a world without problems.
Where everything's easy, and warm, and cosy.
A world I can predict, where riches don't turn to rags
at midnight.
A world of harmony and good feelings.
But it's not like that, Lord.
There are wars and rumours of wars.
Pain and exploitation.
Broken lives on rubbish dumps where hope
lies bleeding.
Lord, I don't understand the way you do things.
With your power, your wisdom, your love,
couldn't you have done it differently? Made it easier?
No, I don't understand.
All the theology in the world doesn't really answer
the question
which bobs up to the surface of my mind
again and again.
And yet – if that's the way it is,
with your power, your wisdom, and love –
maybe that's the way it has to be. For now.

Lord, I know one thing,
and hold it tight through all the storms,
that you will never let me go.
That through the winds of questioning
that blow the leaves of doubt
to drift and build
within the corners of my life
you still stand near, a breath away,
and I await and listen
for the moment
when you call my name.

Lord, in the quietness
reach out and hold me.
Draw me gently into your peace.
And in the loving silence at your heart,
attune my ears
to hear the sounds I never listen to.

The harmony that lies in you,
the discords in the world you've put me in.
The laughter and the tears
in other people's lives.

Make me more sensitive to others' needs.
Sometimes, I hear the words
that others speak,
but fail to grasp their meaning.
Help me to hear the worry
hidden in a throw-away remark,
the fear wrapped in a joke,
the insecurity behind unbending dogmatism.
Let me identify the cry for help
so casually expressed.

Help me to listen more,
and think, and think,
before I speak,
and then to think again.

Winter Walk – *Watercolour*

Part Five:
Rejoicing in Creation

Tanglewood Down – *Watercolour*

I praise you.
Lord of creation.
You spoke the word, and all
things came to be.
Lord of life.
You speak the word, and all
creation lives.
Echoes and shouts with life.
Your life.

Lord, open my eyes
that I may see you in creation power.
Open my heart,
that I may feel your love,
unblocking the arteries of life
to flow without constriction, with life-giving warmth.
Open my mind that I may know the glad certainty,
the daily celebration, of your presence.
Not just in nature's revelation,
but in your son.
One with you when life began,
and one with me as it goes on.
Open my lips,
that I may sing your praises
as I walk the road of faith,
today.

Lord God, Creator,
all life is yours.
All that has come to be
has come through you.
Lives in your energy,
takes breath because you willed it.
Is clothed in your beauty,
your dignity.
Part of your world.
Valued and loved.

Lord, I'm overwhelmed.
It's just too much for me to understand.
Why you,
creator of the galaxies,
the power that spins the planets,
weaves the stars into your tapestry of love
can still have time for me.
I would have thought the universe
would be enough for you.

Lord of the imagination,
spark me into life,
to see the beauty in your world and,
if I can,
inspire me to add
a little beauty of my own.

◆

Teach me to praise you.
Let me see, in this vast universe around me,
your strength and power.
Help me to hear
in the deep reverberations of your creation,
the voice of love and tenderness.
I can't begin to understand,
can never grasp the intricate perfection of
your will.
But I can touch, and feel the warmth.
Lord, let that be enough.

Riches of Summer – *Watercolour*

Thank you for all that makes us different, Lord.
For the variety of your world.
I suppose creation could have been easier
if you'd only chosen one green,
but when I stand in a field and absorb the landscape
there must be a hundred greens, all different.
Light and dark, warm and cold, intense and pale.
That's the beauty, the joy.

Sunlight on the Abbey, Tewkesbury – *Watercolour*

Part Six:
Looking Towards the Future

Sea Mist Norfolk – *Watercolour*

Love is the anchor, Lord.
The one sure thing
that holds me safe.

Lord of the future,
hold out your
hands and
catch me when I jump.

◆

Lord of eternity,
my time is in your hands.
Teach me
to savour every moment.

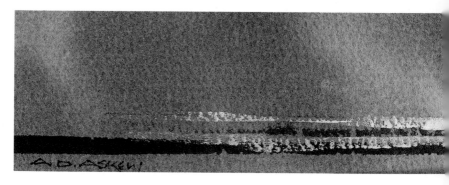

Break in the Clouds, Cornwall – *Watercolour*

There are so many uncertainties, Lord.
So many things to worry about.
People don't seem to get much better
in the way they run things.
but I believe that one day
– although I don't want to waste my time
trying to work out when –
one day
I shall see your power and glory,
when all things are made new.

Love is the anchor, Lord.
The one sure thing
that holds me safe.
I'm bound to you in freedom,
love's paradox.
The tighter that you hold,
the more the space you offer me
to do it in my way.
But always we adventure, you and I,
sail on the ocean,
explore new lands, new roads,
new truth.
And when I'm scared
and feel I've gone too far,
my navigation faulty,
I look around
and you are there beside me.
Telling me
that when the storm clouds gather
and wind whips up,
to blow me in directions
I would not choose to go,

I have no cause to fear.
You are beside me,
yes, but strange,
ahead of me as well.
Love's landmark, beacon blazing,
beckoning me on,
and promising safe anchorage.

Help me to find the courage, Lord,
to launch out into space
wherever you may lead.
To widen my horizons,
soar with confidence,
explore the possibilities
of life and love with you.
Take to the air on wings of faith
and fly.

Lord of eternity.
my time
is in your hands.
Teach me
to savour every moment.

Sunshine and Shadows – *Watercolour*

A.D.ASKEW

Lord, I hear the song, your song.
Faint now and far away,
a whisper on the breeze
playing the leaves of my life,
hardly disturbing them.
But then it grows, your song,
circles the edge of my hearing,
echoes in the empty caverns of my life, enticing,
inviting me to join the choir.
I want to sing your song,
make it my own.
A pilgrim song
which takes me on my way.

I'll sing it when the road is clearly marked,
I'll sing it when my feet are sore
and when my knees begin to ache.

I'll sing it breathlessly
up in the mountains
where the path is full of rocks
and I'm not sure which path to take.

I'll sing it when the clouds roll in
and visibility is nil.
A song of joy and hope and love.
I'll sing it solo if I must
but there are times I hear your voice
and we can sing together.
Sometimes I'll sing it loud and clear,
occasionally I'll whisper it
but, Lord,
I'll go on singing
'til the day
I sing it in your presence
loud and free,
the harmony complete.

Index of first lines